ASIAN ELEPHANTS

Trace Taylor

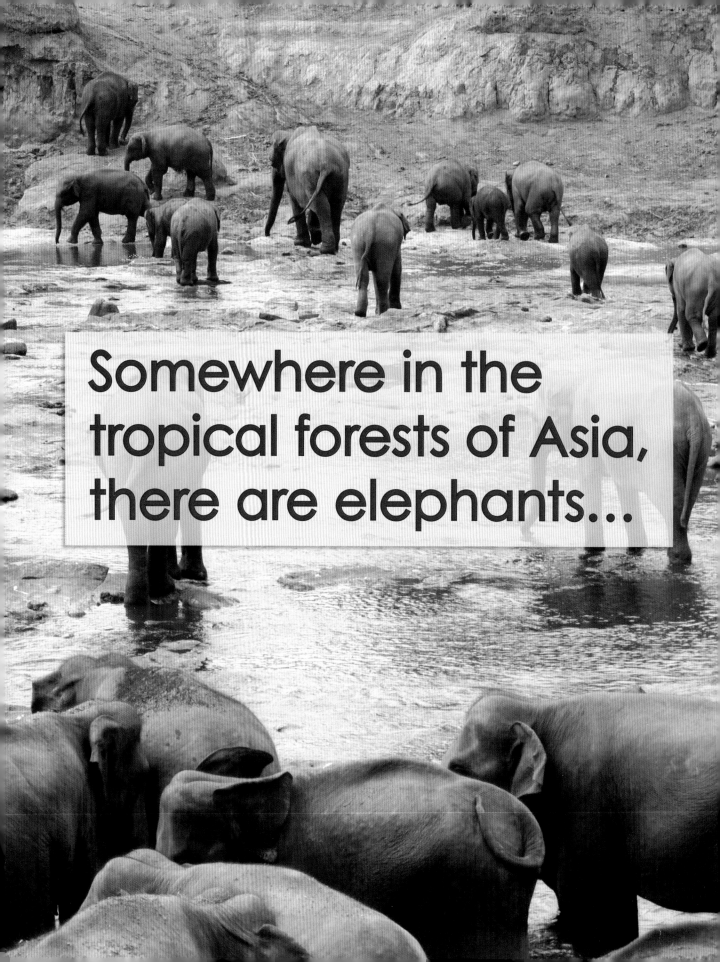

Somewhere in the tropical forests of Asia, there are elephants...

I can see the elephant.  3

 I can see the ears.

I can see the eye.  5

I can see the mouth.

I can see the trunk.

 I can see the nose.

I can see the tusks.

 10 I can see the skin.

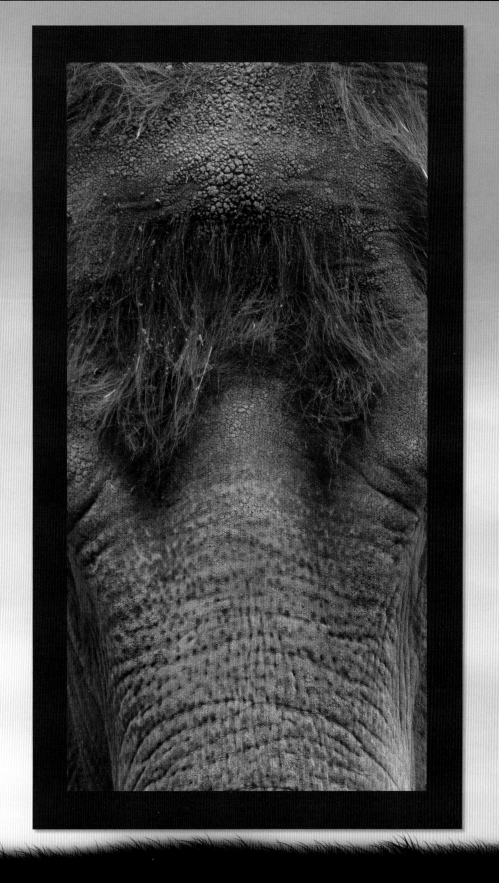

I can see the hair.

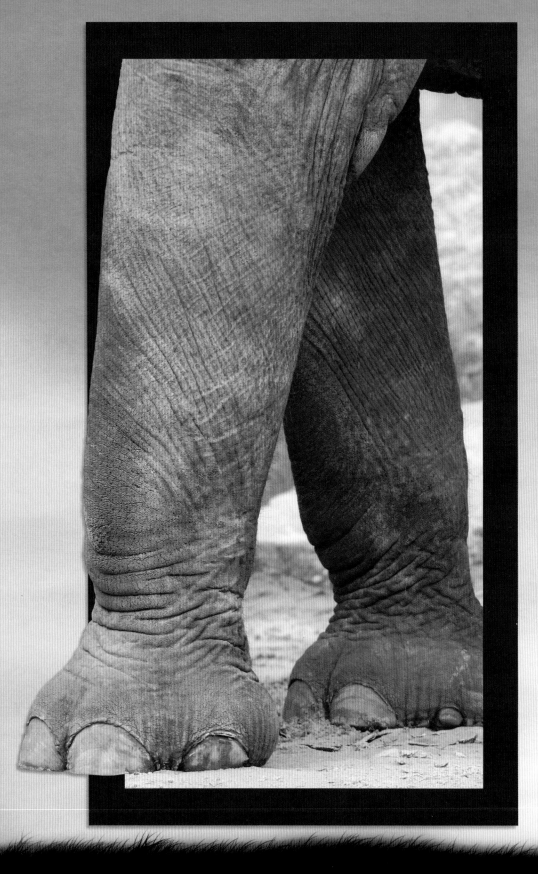

I can see the legs.

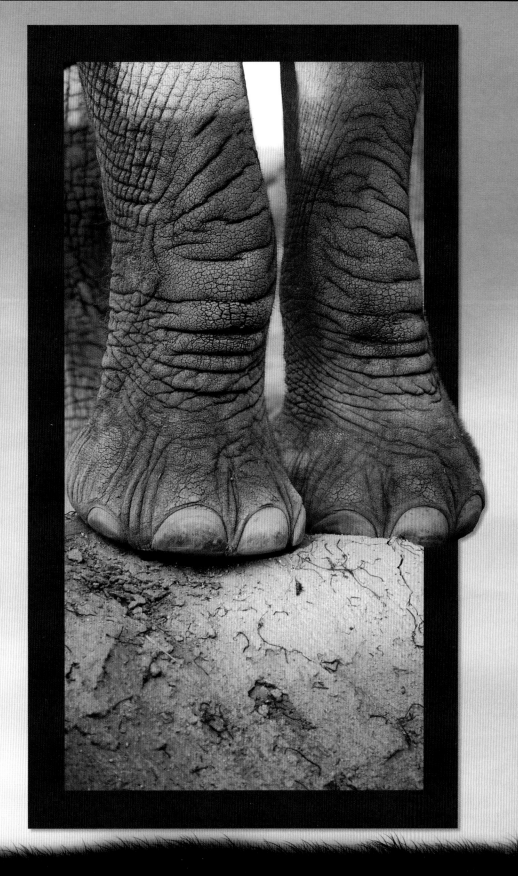

I can see the feet.

  I can see the nails.

I can see the tail.

 I can see the baby.

MORE ABOUT THE ASIAN ELEPHANT

Pinnawala Elephant Orphanage

SIZE CHART

10-foot tall Asian elephant

6-foot tall person

3-foot tall dog

ASIA

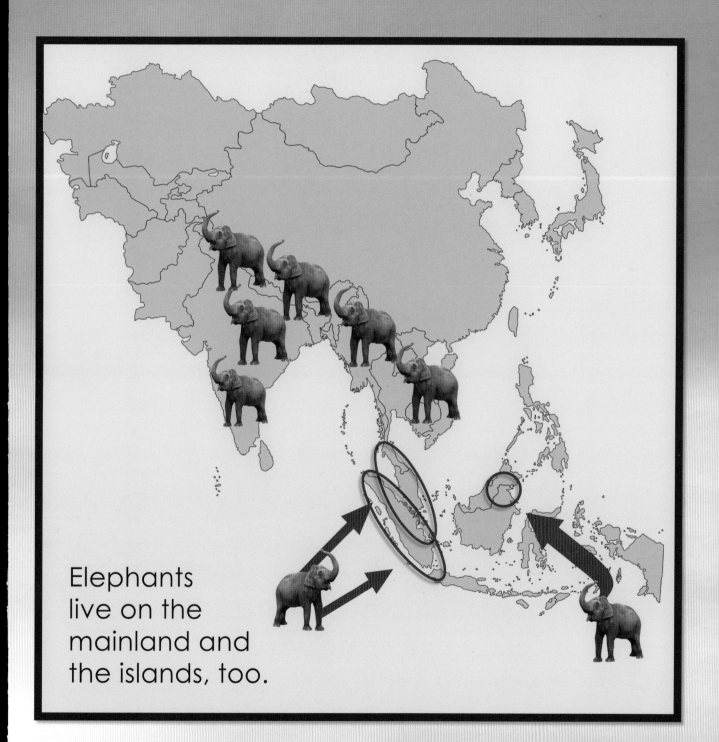

Elephants live on the mainland and the islands, too.

All elephants are good swimmers. Grown elephants begin teaching the baby elephants about water soon after the babies are born. Asian elephants try to stay as close as they can to a source of fresh water.

Asian elephants are not common in the wild now, but many are kept by people as work animals. The elephants go to work each day and play a large role in some Asian cultures. This elephant is getting a bath after a hard day's work.

Pinnawala Elephant Orphanage

I can use the first letter
sound to match the
word to the picture.

tusks

nose

legs

skin

POWER WORDS

How many can you read?

I

can

see

the